SIMPLE SCIENCE EXPERIMENTS

ELECTRICITY AND MAGNETS

Published in 2021 by Enslow Publishing, LLC
101 W. 23rd Street, Suite 240,
New York, NY 10011

Cataloging-in-Publication Data

Names: Oxlade, Chris.
Title: Electricity and magnets / Chris Oxlade.
Description: New York : Enslow Publishing, 2021. | Series: Simple science experiments | Includes glossary and index.
Identifiers: ISBN 9781978520424 (pbk.) | ISBN 9781978520448 (library bound) | ISBN 9781978520431 (6 pack)
Subjects: LCSH: Electricity--Experiments--Juvenile literature. | Magnetism--Experiments--Juvenile literature. | Science--Experiments--Juvenile literature.
Classification: LCC QC527.2 O97 2021 | DDC 537.078--dc23

Printed in the United States of America

CPSIA compliance information: Batch #BS20ENS: For further information contact
Enslow Publishing, New York, New York at 1-800-542-2595

ACKNOWLEDGEMENTS
The publishers would like to thank Shutterstock.com for the use of their photographs: 6 sydeen, 7 Nir Levy, 11(c) Yobidaba, (bl) koya979, (br) Elena Elisseeva
Cover artwork by Paul Boston at Meiklejohn
Every effort has been made to acknowledge the source and copyright holder of each picture.

Publishing Director Belinda Gallagher
Creative Director Jo Cowan
Editors Amanda Askew, Claire Philip
Editorial Assistant Lauren White
Designers Joe Jones, Kayleigh Allen
Cover Designer Rob Hale
Photographer Alex Bibby
Production Elizabeth Collins, Jennifer Brunwin-Jones
Reprographics Stephan Davis, Jennifer Cozens, Rob Hale
Assets Lorraine King

SIMPLE SCIENCE EXPERIMENTS

ELECTRICITY AND MAGNETS

Chris Oxlade

Consultant: John Farndon

CONTENTS

Learn lots about electricity and how it works!

How can you light two bulbs? Find out on page 17.

Experiment time!

Which materials let electricity flow through them? Find out on page 19.

Can a balloon pick up paper? Find out on page 12.

Notes for HELPERS

Help needed

Help and hazards

- All of the experiments are suitable for children to conduct, but they will need help and supervision with some. This is usually because the experiment requires the use of sharp equipment. These experiments are marked with a "Help needed" symbol.

- Read the instructions together before starting and help to assemble the equipment before supervising the experiment.

- It may be useful to carry out your own risk assessment to avoid any possible hazards before the child begins. Check that long hair and any loose clothing are tied back.

- Be careful when handling wire strippers, scissors, or knives, and ensure that wires and nails are stored away safely after use.

Also try... ## Extra experiments

You can also help children with the extra experiments in this book, or search the Internet for more similar ideas. There are hundreds of science experiment websites to choose from.

www.lovemyscience.com This website is packed with simple, fun experiments for children to enjoy.

www.sciencebob.com/experiments/index.php Engaging science experiments with clearly explained instructions will keep kids busy for hours.

www.sciencefun.org/kidszone/experiments You will find lots of entertaining and informative experiments on this colorful, interactive website.

What is ELECTRICITY?

Electricity is a kind of energy, and a major source of power for much of the world. It powers many of the machines we use every day. Electricity is produced in power stations—either by burning coal, oil, or gas—or by using water or nuclear reactors to turn huge turbines.

Creating a flow

Electricity as a power source depends on electrons, which are tiny parts of atoms. When electrons are pushed, they hop from one atom to the next. When billions of electrons are pushed, electricity flows. The push comes from a battery or a power station.

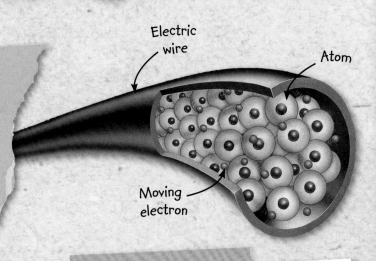

Electric wire

Atom

Moving electron

Materials

Conductors are substances through which electricity can flow. Metals such as copper conduct electricity well.

Insulators are materials, such as wood and plastic, that do not allow electricity to flow.

Electric circuits

An electric circuit is an unbroken loop of conducting material, along which electricity can flow. The three basic parts of an electric circuit are – an energy source such as a battery, a conductor, and an object for the circuit to power, such as a light bulb.

An electric current flows through the copper conductor on the inside of the wire.

The outer covering is made of a plastic insulator, to stop electricity from escaping.

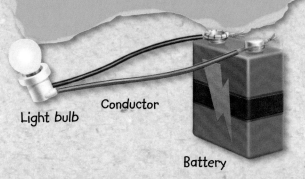

Light bulb

Conductor

Battery

Electricity in ACTION

Electricity is always at work around us – even when we can't see it! This is because all atoms can become electrically charged. Usually the balance between an atom's negatively charged electrons and positively charged center is equal, but if the electrons are lost by being "pushed," the object becomes positively charged. If electrons are gained, the object becomes negatively charged.

Static electricity

This is the buildup of electric charge on a surface. When you rub two materials together, electrons move from one object to the other – leaving one object positively charged and one negatively charged.

After a balloon is rubbed on hair, the hair stands up! Each strand has become positively charged, so they repel and move apart.

Attract or repel

Objects with opposite charges attract each other, and charges that are the same push each other apart (repel).

A negative charge from the cloud meets a positive charge from the ground.

Lightning spark

A lightning flash is a dramatic display of natural electricity. During a thunderstorm, a negative electrical charge builds up at the base of a cloud, while the ground has a positive charge. A lightning spark jumps between them to release the charge.

Magnetic force

Electricity is closely linked with magnetism – the invisible force between magnetic materials. When electricity moves, magnetism is created, and when magnets move, electricity is created. Magnets are pieces of metal that can attract magnetic materials, such as iron.

Around a magnet is a field where its force is felt

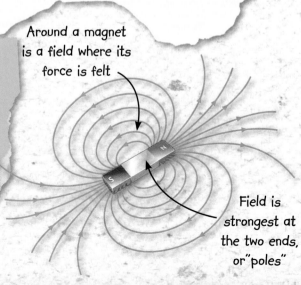

Field is strongest at the two ends, or "poles"

Using this book

Each experiment has numbered instructions and clear explanations about your findings. Read through all the instructions before you start an experiment, and then follow them carefully, one at a time. If you are not sure what to do, ask an adult.

Experiment symbols

① Shows how long the experiment will take once you have collected all the equipment you need.

② Shows if you need to ask an adult to help you with the experiment.

③ Shows how easy or difficult the experiment is to do.

Introduction
See what you will be learning about in each experiment.

Things you will need
You should be able to find the equipment around the house, in a supermarket, or in a hardware store. No special equipment is needed. Always ask before using materials from home.

Safety
If there is a "Help needed" symbol at the start of the experiment, you must ask an adult to help you.

The warning symbol also tells you to be careful when using knives or scissors. Always ask an adult for help.

ELECTRIC balloons

Does your hair sometimes stand on end when you brush or comb it? This is static electricity at work. When different materials rub against each other, electricity jumps from one material to the other.

30 min

Help needed

Easy

You will need
- work surface
- 3 balloons
- wool (sock or glove)
- small scraps of paper (such as tissue paper)
- metal spoon
- cotton thread, 3 ft
- water
- scissors

1a

Blow up a balloon and tie a knot in its neck. Rub the balloon with wool, such as a glove or sock.

1b

Cut the paper into small squares

Move the balloon over the small scraps of paper and watch what happens.

Also try...
Put a charged balloon next to your hair, or near a trickle of water from a tap, and watch what happens.

Q Can a balloon pick up pa...
A Yes, when it has static electricit... surface. Rubbing the balloon with wool a collection of electricity, called static electrici surface. Tiny particles called electrons move wool to the balloon, giving the balloon a nega charge. This negative charge attracts positiv charges in the paper. As the pieces of pape small, the pull is big enough to pick them u

Also try...
Simple mini experiments to test the science you've learned.

Stages

Numbers and letters guide you through the stages of each experiment.

Doing the experiments

✳ Clear a surface to work on, such as a table, and cover it with newspaper if you need to.

✳ You could wear an apron or an old T-shirt to protect your clothing.

✳ Gather all the equipment you need before you start, and tidy up after each experiment.

✳ Ask an adult to help you when an experiment is marked with a "Help needed" or warning symbol.

✳ Work over a tray or sink when you are pouring water.

✳ Always ask an adult to help if you are unsure what to do.

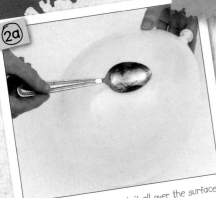

2a

Wet a metal spoon and rub it all over the surface of the balloon.

Blow up two more balloons. Tie the end of the cotton thread to the neck of one of them, then rub both balloons all over with wool.

2b

Now test the effect of this by moving the balloon over the pieces of paper again. What happens this time?

3b

Don't let the balloons touch each other

Ask a helper to hold the top of the length of thread, letting the balloon hang down. Move the other balloon towards it. Watch what happens to the hanging balloon.

Labels

Handy labels will provide you with useful tips and information to help your experiment run smoothly.

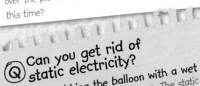

Q Can you get rid of static electricity?

A Yes, rubbing the balloon with a wet spoon removes its charge. The static electricity on the balloon's surface flows away into the spoon (the water helps this happen by improving the metal's contact with the balloon). Now the balloon has no charge, so it can no longer attract the bits of paper.

Q Can balloons push each other?

A Yes, static electricity pushes the balloons apart. Rubbing the two balloons with wool creates static electricity on the surfaces of the balloons. The charges on both are negative. Charges that are the same (two positive or two negative) always push each other away (repel), so the balloons are pushed apart.

13

Explanation

At the end of each experiment is a question-and-answer explanation. It tells you what should have happened and why.

Scientist KIT

Before you begin experimenting you will need to gather some equipment. You should be able to find all of it around the house, from a local supermarket or from a hardware store. Ask an adult's permission before using anything and take care when you see a warning sign.

Electrical bits

- 1.5V AA battery
- 1.5V flashlight bulbs (not LED bulbs)
- copper wire
- thin, insulated electrical wire
- wire strippers (or pliers)

Battery

⚠ Warning!

Although it is very useful in everyday life, electricity can be dangerous. It can give off shocks and is particularly dangerous when near water.

Copper wire

From the Kitchen

- aluminum drink can (empty)
- glass
- glass jar
- jug
- aluminum foil
- kitchen paper
- knife
- plastic tray
- scissors
- sieve
- spoons (metal)
- table salt
- tea towel
- water

Aluminum foil

Glove

From the craft box

- cotton thread
- pen
- small scraps of paper, such as tissue paper
- tape
- wool (sock or glove)

Scissors

Tissue paper

⚠ Warning!

Scissors and knives are extremely sharp and can cut you easily. Make sure you ask an adult for help. When passing scissors or a knife, always point the blunt end towards the other person.

Handy hint!

You can get small scraps of paper from a hole punch. They all will be the same shape, and you will be reusing otherwise unwanted paper!

Other stuff

- balloons
- bar magnet
- clothespin
- compass
- copper coin
- large steel nail (or screw)
- masking tape or plastic insulating tape
- paper clips
- plastic document wallet
- short, thick rubber band
- talcum powder
- various objects made from different materials, such as paper, wood, glass, plastic, metal
- zinc-coated (galvanized) nail

Clothespin

Balloon

Handy hint!
You could draw silly faces on the balloons using a felt-tip pen. Make sure you wait for the ink to dry before rubbing the balloon with wool.

Copper coins

Places you'll need to work

- work surface

Electrical wire

Remember to recycle and reuse

One way to help the environment is by recycling and reusing materials such as glass, paper, plastics, and scrap metals. It is mostly cheaper and less wasteful than making new products from stratch.

Reusing means you use materials again in their original form rather than throwing them away.

Recycling is when materials are taken to a plant where they can be melted and remade into either the same or new products.

Handy hint!
Most drink cans are made of aluminum and can be recycled. Many supermarkets now have recycling points where you can dispose of your empty cans.

ELECTRIC
balloons

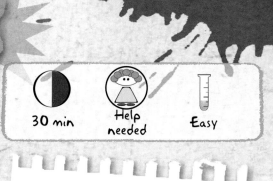

Does your hair sometimes stand on end when you brush or comb it? This is static electricity at work. When different materials rub against each other, electricity jumps from one material to the other.

30 min | Help needed | Easy

You will need

- work surface
- 3 balloons
- wool (sock or glove)
- small scraps of paper (such as tissue paper)
- metal spoon
- cotton thread, 3 ft
- water
- scissors

1a

Blow up a balloon and tie a knot in its neck. Rub the balloon with wool, such as a glove or sock.

1b

Cut the paper into small squares

Move the balloon over the small scraps of paper and watch what happens.

Also try...

Put a charged balloon next to your hair, or near a trickle of water from a tap, and watch what happens.

Q Can a balloon pick up paper?

A Yes, when it has static electricity on its surface. Rubbing the balloon with wool creates a collection of electricity, called static electricity, on the surface. Tiny particles called electrons move from the wool to the balloon, giving the balloon a negative charge. This negative charge attracts positive electric charges in the paper. As the pieces of paper are small, the pull is big enough to pick them up.

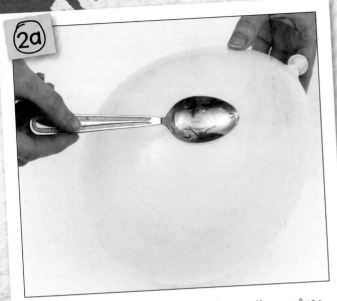

2a

Wet a metal spoon and rub it all over the surface of the balloon.

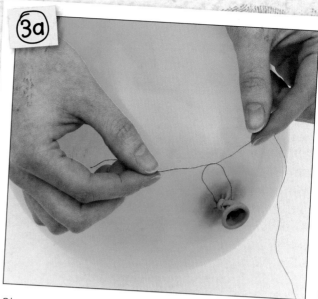

3a

Blow up two more balloons. Tie the end of the cotton thread to the neck of one of them, then rub both balloons all over with wool.

2b

Now test the effect of this by moving the balloon over the pieces of paper again. What happens this time?

3b

Don't let the balloons touch each other

Ask a helper to hold the top of the length of thread, letting the balloon hang down. Move the other balloon towards it. Watch what happens to the hanging balloon.

Q Can you get rid of static electricity?

A Yes, rubbing the balloon with a wet spoon removes its charge. The static electricity on the balloon's surface flows away into the spoon (the water helps this happen by improving the metal's contact with the balloon). Now the balloon has no charge, so it can no longer attract the bits of paper.

Q Can balloons push each other?

A Yes, static electricity pushes the balloons apart. Rubbing the two balloons with wool creates static electricity on the surfaces of the balloons. The charges on both are negative. Charges that are the same (two positive or two negative) always push each other away (repel), so the balloons are pushed apart.

STATIC patterns

Some photocopiers and computer printers use static electricity to work. The static makes the marks you see on the finished page. Get ready to find out how this process works.

30 min

No help needed

Easy

You will need
- work surface
- plastic document wallet
- talcum powder
- sieve
- masking tape or plastic insulating tape
- plastic tray
- paper towel
- water
- scissors

a Shake some talcum powder through a sieve onto a plastic tray. The sieve helps to spread the talcum powder more evenly.

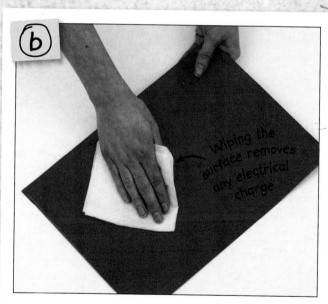

b Moisten a paper towel with water and wipe it over both sides of your plastic document wallet. Then, dry the plastic thoroughly with a dry paper towel. This will remove any static electricity from the surface of the plastic.

Wiping the surface removes any electrical charge

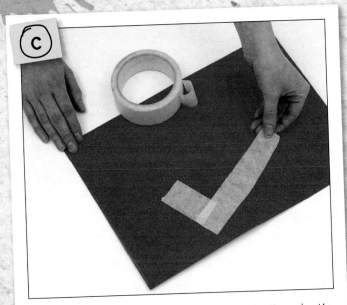

Cut pieces of tape and stick them onto the plastic to make a shape, such as a check mark. Press the tape down firmly onto the plastic, but fold over the end to make it easy to rip off.

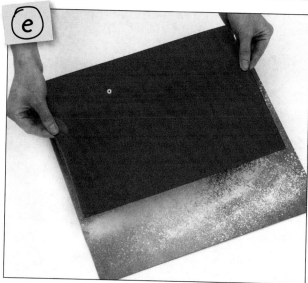

Turn the plastic over, but don't put it down. Very carefully hold it over the tray and lower it slowly, until it is just above the talcum powder.

Now you are ready to make your pattern. Put the plastic on a table and quickly rip off the pieces of tape.

Turn the plastic over to see what's happened.

Q Can I make a shape in talcum powder?

A **Yes, using static electricity.** Ripping the tape quickly off the plastic document wallet creates static electricity where the tape was stuck down. This happens because the tape and plastic are made from different materials. The electric charge attracts the tiny particles of talcum powder to the plastic, making your shape.

Simple electric CIRCUITS

A flashlight makes light using electricity. How does it work? This experiment shows how electricity flows around a loop to make the bulb light.

15 min | No help needed | Easy

You will need

- work surface
- 1.5V AA battery
- short, thick rubber band
- scissors
- 3 lengths of aluminum foil, 8 in x 1 in
- 2 1.5V flashlight bulbs (not LED bulbs)

Preparation: Make a circuit

a Fold each of the pieces of foil in half twice, lengthways, to make thin strips of foil.

Put the small rubber band lengthways around the battery so that it goes over both metal terminals of the battery.

b

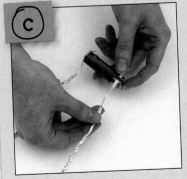

c Put one end of each foil strip under the rubber band at each end of the battery. Make sure the two strips don't touch, otherwise an electric current will flow.

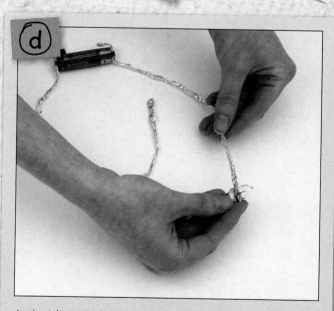

d

A flashlight *bulb* has two terminals (contacts). One is the metal casing below the base of the glass (the screw thread or bayonet prongs); the other is on the bottom. Wrap the end of one of the foil strips around the metal casing and twist it to make it stay in place. Make sure the strip does not touch the contact at the bottom of the bulb.

① If the bulb slips out of the foil, hold the foil down with tape

Press the bottom contact of your bulb onto the other foil strip.

②a Wrap the second piece of foil around the metal casing of the second bulb.

②b Place the third piece of foil on your work surface.

②c Third piece of foil

Put the bottom contacts of each bulb (which are connected to the battery with foil strips) onto the third piece of foil. What happens?

Ⓠ How does a battery light a bulb?

Ⓐ By connecting the bulb to the battery with the foil strips, you make a loop called a circuit. Electricity flows around the circuit. This flow is called an electric current. The battery is like a pump that pushes the current around the circuit. The current comes out of the terminal marked + (positive) and goes into the terminal marked − (negative). As the current goes through the bulb, it glows.

③ Wrap the second bulb in the same piece of foil as the first bulb

Take the foil strip with the bulb attached and wrap it around the side contact of the second bulb, further down. Press the bottom contacts of the bulbs against the other strip.

Ⓠ Can you make the two bulbs glow brighter?

Ⓐ Yes, by sending the electricity through both bulbs at the same time, not one after the other. We say that the bulbs are connected in "parallel."

Ⓠ How can you light two bulbs?

Ⓐ By putting the bulbs in "series." The electricity flows from the battery, through one bulb, then through the other bulb, and back to the battery. The light from the bulbs is quite dim.

CONDUCTORS
and insulators

Some materials let electricity pass through them easily. Others don't let electricity pass through them at all. Here's an experiment to find out which materials are which.

15 min   No help needed   Easy

Preparation: Make a circuit

See page 16 for how to make your basic circuit. You'll only need two lengths of foil.

You will need

- 1.5V AA battery
- short, thick rubber band
- 1.5V flashlight bulb (not LED bulb)
- 2 lengths of aluminum foil, 8 in x 1 in
- scissors
- paper
- pen
- objects made from various materials, such as paper, wood, glass, plastic, metal

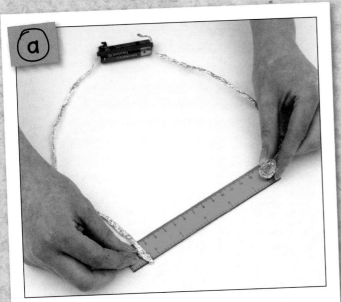

a

Touch the base of the bulb and the end of the second foil strip on either end of a plastic ruler or pen. What happens to the bulb?

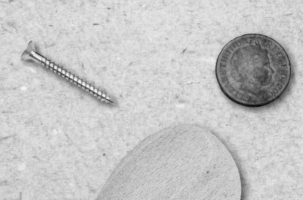

Repeat step a using other objects. Each time, write down the name of the object and its material in a results table. Put an X next to it if the bulb does not light up, and a check mark if it does.

OBJECT	MATERIAL	X	✓
Pen	Plastic	X	
Ruler	Plastic		
Paper clip	Metal		
Book	Paper		
Pencil	Wood		

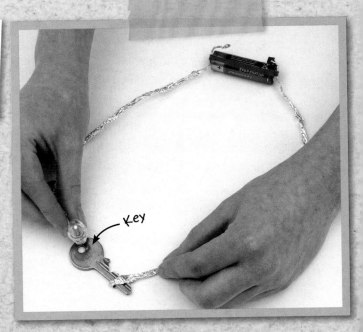

key

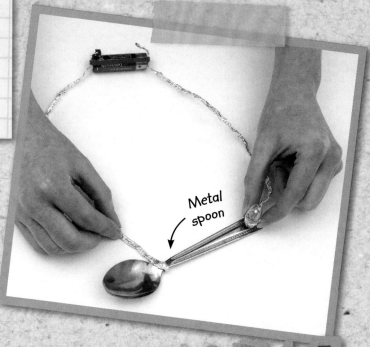

Metal spoon

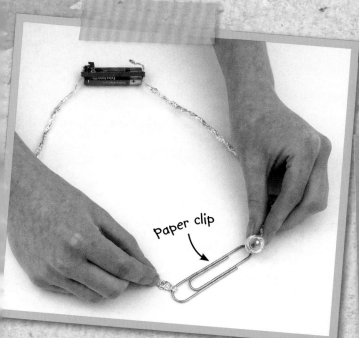

Paper clip

Q Which materials let electricity flow through them?

A Metals let electricity flow through them, lighting up the bulb. Metals are conductors. Other materials, including paper, wood, and plastic, don't let electricity flow through them. They are insulators.

19

DETECTING electricity

30 min | Help needed | Tricky

How can we tell if electricity is flowing along a wire? You need a detector, such as a compass. A compass needle moves when it is near a wire with electricity flowing through it.

You will need

- 1.5V AA battery
- short, thick rubber band
- thin insulated electrical wire, 7 ft
- 1.5V flashlight bulb (not LED bulb)
- sticky tack
- scissors
- 2 lengths of aluminum foil, 8 in x 1 in
- tape
- wire strippers or a knife
- compass

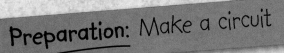

Preparation: Make a circuit

See page 16 for how to make your basic circuit. You'll only need two lengths of foil.

1a

Put the compass on top of one of the foil strips, then touch the strip with the bottom contact of the bulb. This completes the circuit and makes the bulb light up.

1b

Now remove the bulb to turn the light off. What happens to the compass needle?

Q Can you detect current?

A Yes, the compass needle detects the current. When electricity flows along the foil, it turns the foil into a weak magnet. This makes the compass needle, which is also a magnet, twitch.

Preparation: Strip some wire

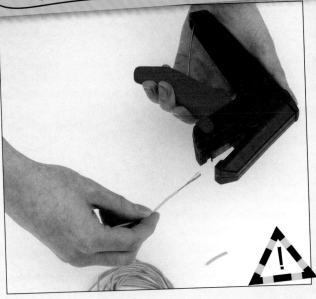

Ask an adult to strip 1 inch of insulation from either end of the insulated electrical wire. This can be done with wire strippers or a sharp knife.

Preparation: Make a current detector

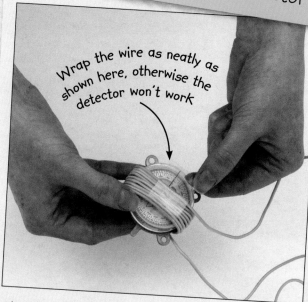

Wrap the wire as neatly as shown here, otherwise the detector won't work

Starting about 8 inches from one end of the wire, wrap the wire around your compass. Finish winding it about 8 inches from the other end. Use tape and sticky tack to keep the wire in place.

Ⓠ **Can I make the detector more sensitive?**

Ⓐ **Yes, by wrapping wire around the compass.** This turns the compass into a much stronger magnet when the circuit is complete and electricity is flowing through the wire. The stronger magnet makes the compass needle more sensitive to the flow of electricity.

②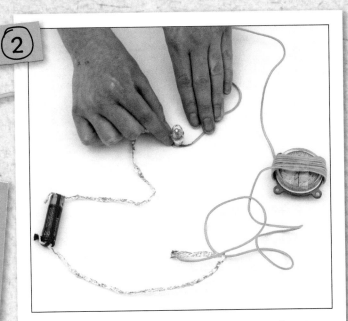

Attach one bare wire end to one of the foil strips, and the other end to the bottom contact of the bulb. Electricity will flow through the wire. Is the compass needle moving differently now?

Battery POWER

All sorts of electric gadgets need a battery to work. A battery is a source of electricity. Batteries make electricity from chemicals. In this experiment, you can see how this happens.

30 min   Help needed   Tricky

You will need

- copper coin or copper wire
- zinc-coated (galvanized) nail or screw
- table salt
- glass
- clothespin
- tape
- wire strippers or a knife
- jug
- water
- teaspoon
- 2 lengths of thin insulated electrical wire, 20 in long
- 1 length of thin insulated electrical wire, 7 ft long

Preparation: Strip some wire

See page 21 for how to strip wire. You'll need two pieces of wire about 20 inches long.

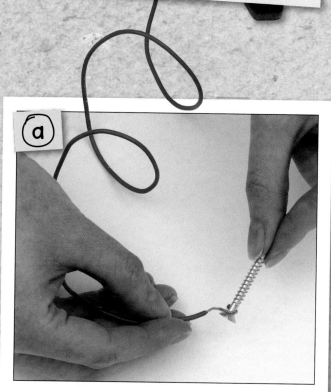

a

Wrap the stripped end of one of the wires tightly around the screw, just under the screw's head.

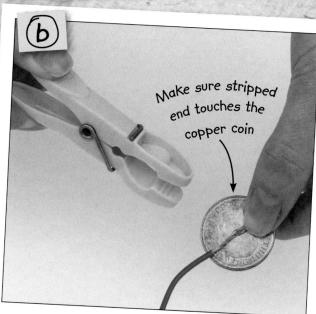

b

Make sure stripped end touches the copper coin

Put the stripped end of the second wire on top of the copper coin and hold it on using a clothespin.

Preparation: Make a current detector

See page 21 for how to make a current detector.

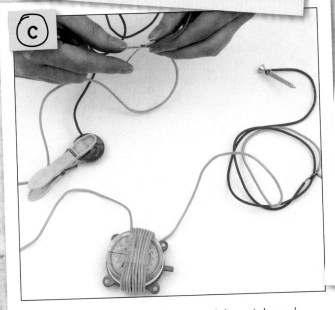

Twist together each of the remaining stripped ends of the two insulated wires to the ends of the current detector. Using tape, attach the current detector to your work surface (to stop it from moving around later).

Fill a glass with water and stir in a couple of teaspoons of table salt. Put the screw underwater in the glass.

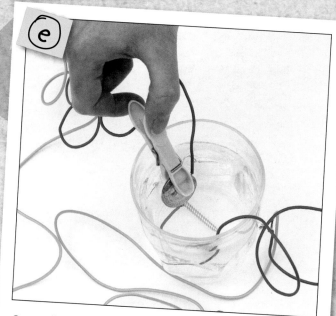

Carefully lower the coin into the water (don't let the coin touch the screw). As you do this, watch the needle on the current detector very closely. What happens? Take the clothespin out again – what happens?

Q Can coins and screws make electricity?

A Yes, by putting them in salty water. The screw and the coin are made of two different metals (the screw is coated in zinc and the coin is copper). The water contains tiny particles with an electric charge. The different metals make the particles move through the water, and this makes an electric current – you should've seen the current detector twitch slightly as electricity was generated. Batteries work in a similar way.

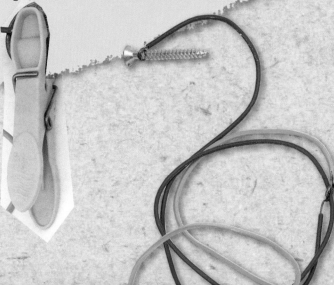

MAGIC
magnet

This experiment shows that electricity can be used to make a magnet that will pick up small metal objects. The magnet can be switched on and off.

 15 min

 Help needed

 Tricky

You will need

- work surface
- large steel nail (or screw)
- thin insulated electrical wire, 3 ft
- 1.5V AA battery
- sticky tack
- paper clips
- tape
- wire strippers or a knife
- short, thick rubber band

Preparation: Strip some wire

See page 21 for how to strip wire. You'll need two pieces of wire about three feet long.

Preparation: Make an electromagnet

Put sticky tack on the nail first to help hold the wire in place

Starting about 4 inches from one end of the wire, wrap the wire tightly around the length of the nail up to the nail's head.

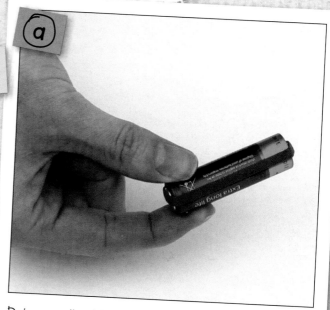

(a)

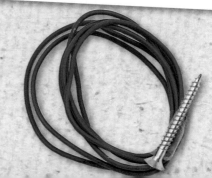

Put a small rubber band lengthways around the battery so that it goes over both metal terminals.

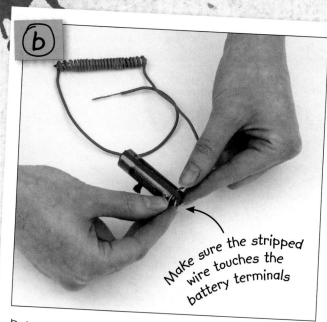

(b)

Make sure the stripped wire touches the battery terminals

Put each of the stripped ends of the wire from the electromagnet under the rubber band at each end of the battery.

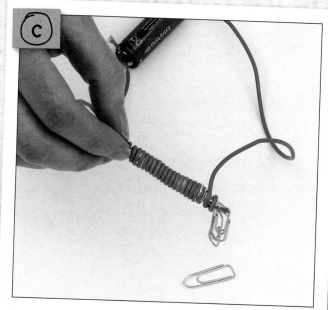

(c)

Put a few paper clips on the work surface. Hold the electromagnet with the pointy end of the nail close to the paper clips. Watch what happens to the paper clips. Don't leave the wire connected to the battery for more than a few seconds at a time, otherwise the battery will quickly run down and become hot.

(d)

After a few seconds, take one of the wires away from the battery. What happens to the paper clips now?

Q Can electricity pick up a paper clip?

A Yes, the electricity turns the nail or screw into an electromagnet. The electromagnet pulls on the paper clips because they are made of steel. When you take the wire away from the battery, the electricity stops flowing, so the electromagnet stops working and the paper clips fall back to the table.

Also try...

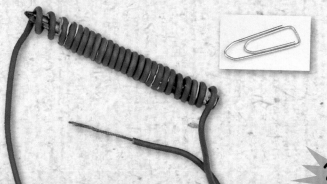

Make an electromagnet using twice as much wire. Add another battery in series with the first, using another piece of foil to connect the two batteries end to end (make sure both are the same way around). Adding more wire and more batteries should make the electromagnet stronger. Can you pick up more paper clips now?

Buzz!
BUZZ!

Using an electromagnet, you can create a noise by making and breaking a circuit. This experiment shows you how to build a buzzer.

30 min   Help needed   Hard

Preparation: Make a circuit

See page 16 for how to make your basic circuit. You'll only need one piece of foil, and only follow stages a, b, and c.

You will need

- work surface
- medium-sized metal paper clip
- tape
- empty aluminum drink can
- scissors
- 1.5V AA battery
- short, thick rubber band
- one length of aluminum foil, 8 in x 1 in
- large steel nail
- thin insulated electrical wire, 3 ft
- wire strippers or a knife

Preparation: Make an electromagnet

See page 24 for how to make an electromagnet.

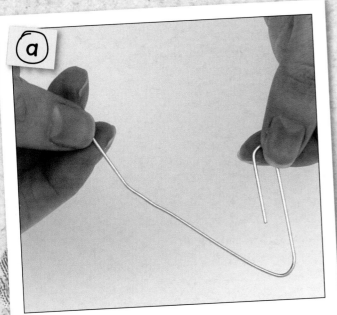

(a)

Straighten out the first two bends of the paper clip, so you have a straight piece of wire with a hook at one end.

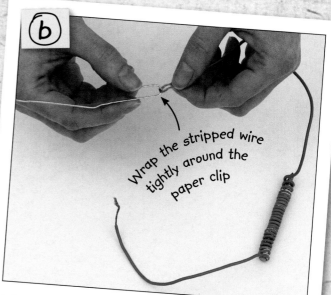

(b)

Wrap the stripped wire tightly around the paper clip

Wrap the end of one of the stripped wires from the electromagnet around the bend of the hook in the clip.

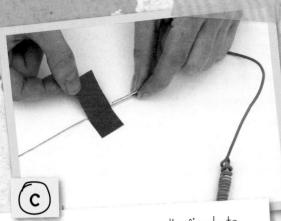

c Tape the loop in the paper clip firmly to your work surface. Gently bend it upwards so that the straight end is about 1 inch above the work surface.

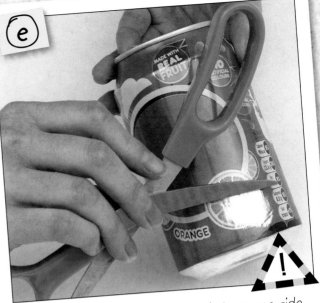

Ask an adult to scrape off the ink from one side of the can to make a patch of bare metal. Tape the spare end of the foil strip (attached to the battery) to the underside of the can.

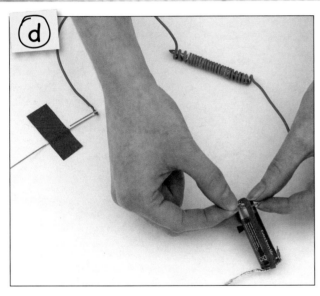

d Put the spare stripped end of the electromagnet under the rubber band at one end of the battery, touching the terminal.

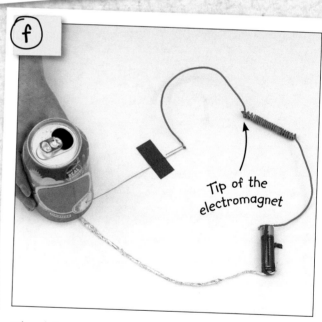

Tip of the electromagnet

Stand the can next to the straightened paper clip so that the end just touches the bare metal patch on the can.

Q Can an electromagnet make noise?

A Yes, by making a buzzer. The parts of the buzzer make an electric circuit. The electricity flows from the battery, through the can, along the paper clip, through the electromagnet, and back to the battery. When the electromagnet is moved closer to the paper clip, it pulls the tip of the clip away from the can. This breaks the circuit, which turns off the electromagnet. As electricity stops flowing, the paper clip springs back to touch the can and reconnects the circuit. This happens again and again, making a buzzing noise.

g Move the pointy end of the electromagnet slowly towards the center of the straight part of the paper clip and listen carefully. What can you hear? If it doesn't work, adjust the distance between the electromagnet and the paper clip.

MAGIC moving wire

Some of the other experiments in this book showed how electricity can make magnets, and wires with electricity in them make magnets move. In this experiment, you can see how electricity and magnets can make a wire move.

30 min | Help needed | Hard

Preparation: Make a circuit

See page 16 for how to make your basic circuit. You'll only need two pieces of foil, and only follow stages a, b, and c.

You will need

- work surface
- 1.5V AA battery
- 2 lengths of aluminum foil, 8 in x 1 in
- short, thick rubber band
- 3 lengths copper wire, 1/4 x 2 in, 1 x 5 in
- bar magnet
- wire strippers, knife, or pliers
- tape
- scissors

a

Tape the two long pieces of copper wire to your work surface, parallel to each other, about 2 inches apart.

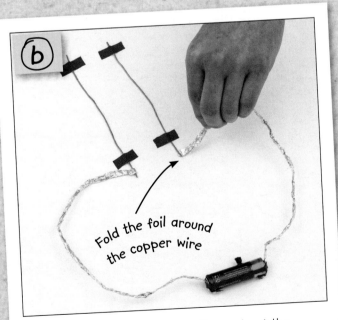

b

Fold the foil around the copper wire

Take your circuit, and attach the ends of the foil strips to the copper wire.

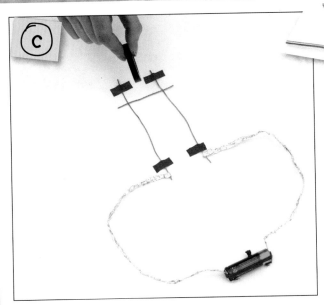

Put the shorter piece of copper wire across the two longer wires, completing the electric circuit. Hold one end of the magnet just above the center of the shorter wire, and watch what happens. Don't leave the shorter wire in place for long, as it will quickly make the battery run down.

Q Can a magnet move a copper wire?

A Yes, if a magnet is placed near a wire that has an electric current running through it. When electricity flows through the copper wire, it becomes a magnet itself. The bar magnet creates a magnetic field around the copper wire. This pushes the wire, so it rolls along. This is called the motor effect. All electric motors use this to work.

As the short piece of copper wire moves, the electric circuit stays intact

Also try...

Turn the magnet around so the opposite end is near the wire. The wire should move in the opposite direction it did before because you are using the opposite pole of the magnet. Now try swapping the pieces of foil, so they touch opposite terminals on the battery. The wire should move the opposite way too, because the electricity flows in the opposite direction through the wire.

Electricity with SALT

Some liquids let electricity flow through them. In this experiment you can see how electricity flows through salty water.

 15 min

 No help needed

 Tricky

You will need

- work surface
- glass
- 1.5V AA battery
- short, thick rubber band
- table salt
- thin insulated electrical wire, 7 ft
- 2 lengths of aluminum foil, 8 in x 1 in
- tape
- wire strippers or a knife
- scissors
- compass
- water

Preparation: Make a circuit

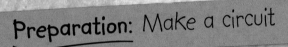

See page 16 for how to make your basic circuit. You'll only need one piece of foil, and only follow stages a, b, and c.

Preparation: Make a current detector

See page 21 for how to make a current detector.

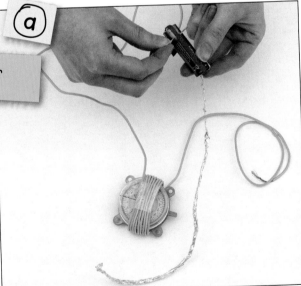

(a)

Put one of the stripped wire ends from the current detector under the rubber band at one end of the battery (attached to the foil strip on the circuit).

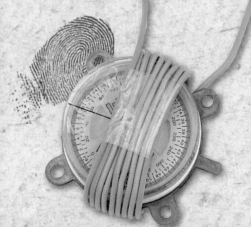

Fill the glass with water. Fold the spare end of the foil (attached to the battery) over the lip of the glass, so that the last few inches are in the water. In the same way, fold a spare strip of foil over the lip of the glass.

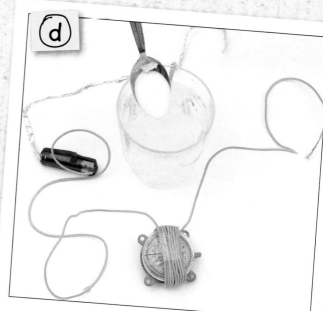

Add a teaspoon of salt to the water in the jar and gently stir it in. Repeat step c again. What happens this time?

Attach the second strip of foil to the spare stripped end of the electricity detector. What happens to the compass needle?

Q Can salt make electricity flow?

A Yes, when you add salt to the water, more electricity flows. The compass needle in the current detector twitches if the wire touches the foil, because the circuit is complete. With plain water in the jar, only a tiny amount of electricity flows. When you add salt, the amount of electricity increases, so the needle twitches more. This happens because the salt breaks into tiny particles that are charged with electricity, which then carries the electricity through the water.

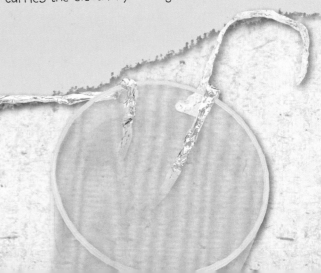

GLOSSARY

Attract To draw two objects with opposite charges together (opposite of repel).

Charge A property that causes particles to attract or repel each other. Objects can have either a positive or negative charge.

Circuit A loop through which electricity can flow.

Conductor A material, such as copper, which allows the flow of an electrical current.

Detector A device that recognizes the presence of electricity in a circuit.

Electromagnet A strong magnet that is only magnetic when an electric current passes through it.

Insulator A material, such as rubber, that does not conduct electricity.

Magnetic field The area around a magnet inside which its magnetic force can be detected. An electric current creates a magnetic field.

Negative charge When a substance is negatively charged, it gains electrons.

Parallel circuit A circuit where an equal amount of electricity flows through two objects, such as light bulbs, at the same time.

Positive charge When a substance becomes positively charged, it loses electrons.

Repel To push two objects with the same charge away from each other (opposite of attract).

Series circuit A circuit where electricity flows through one object, such as a light bulb, and then on to another object.

Terminal The ends of a battery. One is positive and one is negative.

INDEX